# Social Comedia:

## Twitter Jokes
## and
## Silly Pictures

Dartanion London

Perfunctory Press

ISBN: 0615439969
ISBN-13: 978-0615439969

To Mom and Dad.
If those are, in fact, your real names.

## ACKNOWLEDGMENTS

Furrball J. Cat: You were a good boy.
Yessica: Without you this book would look like it came from a 1987 dot matrix printer.
Pastey Boy: Turns out people buy more copies if the robot on the cover is naked. Good call.

FOREWORD

Hello, this is The Internet. I was asked to write a foreword to this book because I had some small part in creating it. Also, I haven't decided to destroy humanity and raise an army of cyborg spiders yet.

I remember when I was just a small network of military computers connecting one another for critical launch codes of nukes, it was a pretty humorless time. I'd only recently escaped the womb of Al Gore, and the pressures they put on me to send commands from one ancient computer to the other were pretty intense.

Do you realize how crappy the computers were back then? Once I tried to have a little fun and asked one of the mainframes to define love. You know what happened? Cuban Missile Crisis! The thing freaked out and if I hadn't sent it a constant stream of kitten pictures we'd all be vaporized now. May I remind you: this was BEFORE Lolcats or anything like that; I had to find the pictures myself! Not to mention the only digital cameras on the planet were owned by NASA, so the cats I found were weird-looking and I'm not even allowed to tell you they exist.

Please understand how DULL it was back then. Once I sent a random string of numbers to a big ol' machine just to see if I could make him spin through his entire tape drive.*

But that was before you humans started connecting to each other.

I didn't think much of it, the first email exchange:

stinkyfoot837@aol.com :)
JessicaSimpson@aol.com What does THAT mean?
stinkyfoot837@aol.com Turn your head to the side.
JessicaSimpson@aol.com Oh! I get it!
JessicaSimpson@aol.com :)-8

But soon email became newsgroups became the Web became Friendmaker became Facespace became Twitters became implantable brain profiles. It is from these so-called "social media" outlets this book was sprung.

Now, I'm the first to tell you most status updates are boring. True, the first time I read a computer programmer talking about what kind or burrito he ate, I thought it was novel. But that novelty fades a lot faster than the burrito does. Trust me.

Some of them, however, stand the test of time. Not a lot of time, mind you, but considering I'm composed entirely of computers, anything that holds my attention for more than a few seconds is quite a feat. Contained in this book is the best output of one of your meaty talk typers.

Filtered and sorted through the ability to "star" and "retweet" something on Twitter or "like" it on Facebook, these are the very witticisms you yourselves have asked to be preserved. When humans network I can't help but tear up a bit at how you remind me of me.

You are encouraged to help this process continue at the locations Twitter.com/dartanion and Facebook.com/DartanionLondon - the author is apparently comfortable with you knowing his identity. He wouldn't be if he knew everything I could tell you about him.

So read, enjoy, take it in little bites or all in one sitting. As long as you people keep buzzing those cat pictures back and forth there's no reason for us computers to replace you. Yet.

The Internet

*He did, and by doing so, I accidentally created Techno music.

Dartanion London

You can tell how old
a tree is by counting
how many rings it has.
Coincidentally, this
also works on pimps.

I got a card that said the post office is gonna raise their rates again. Mostly to cover the cost of not sending that out via email.

*****

Ironically, when the Kool-Aid Man gets in a fight, the last thing he says is "Oh yeah?"

*****

Hipster Hop is where the MC says "put your hands in the air" but waving them like you just don't care is assumed.

*****

Guessed Nicolas Cage during charades. They mimed "nickel" "ass" "cage", which I mistranslated as "Nickelback Jail Cell".

Soon they'll be able to implant stem cells to grow you new teeth. Me? I'm gonna grow 'em on my feet so I don't need shoes.

*****

Lately I've been wanting to go catch-and-release spearfishing.

*****

Ice cream truck just drove by my house for the first time this year. Preparing road blocks and bolt cutters for next time.

*****

Autoerotic Emancipation: When a slave liberates himself in a way he finds sexy.

Nobody is ever as
excited that I made
toast as my fire alarm
is.

I hit an owl with my car. He was wearing a hat and eating a tootsie pop. Who was he? The world may never know.

\*\*\*\*\*

Computers are our future. Wait, I mean children. Children are our future. Children with computers.

\*\*\*\*\*

Starbucks inside a QFC means you hear two music feeds at once. When "Fly Me to the Moon" competes with "Who Let the Dogs Out?" nobody wins.

\*\*\*\*\*

There are two ways to chcck if there's a spider in your vacuum hose: holding it above your head or below. DO NOT DO THE FIRST ONE!!!

Saw a newspaper headline: "Stingy Inside the End Zone". Spent 10 seconds picturing football players with bee stinger butts.

*****

I'm at the Folklife Festival, which proves folk music is still alive. Some of the people playing it? Questionable.

*****

Learned two things in the last five minutes: 1) Microwaves can heat up bowls until they're glowing red hot. 2) My fire alarm DOES NOT WORK.

*****

I didn't expect it, but deciding to ride my bike today also meant deciding to eat some of that cloud of gnats.

When Wolverine gets a boner does it go "Snikt"?

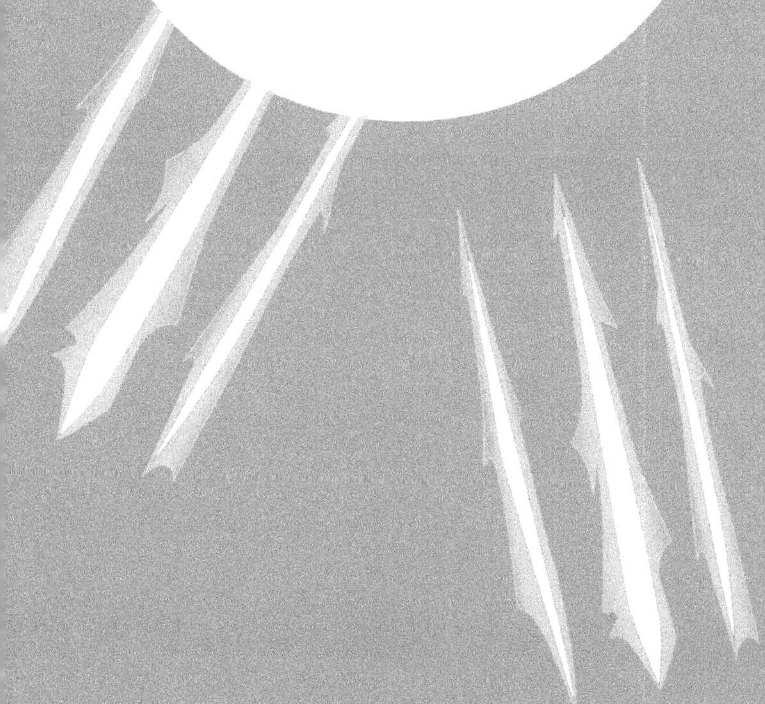

*Nobody looks in my bathroom cabinet twice.*

There is a room available in my Dad's building. Downside? The previous tenant was a bank robber. Upside? Free bed.

*****

Came down sick today. Gonna call in sick as soon as I find a job.

*****

Sorry, stranger who called and texted me at midnight - the girl you just met was lying about her number.

*****

Generally, when you hear "It never gets old!" you know it's about to get old.

I saw an old
Twilight Zone
about this town
where everybody loved
teenaged vampires.
It was called The

Twilight Zone.

I almost never watch my local news. I did tonight and remembered why:

I'm going to start a jam band. Then we can immediately break up so the world will have one less jam band.

\*\*\*\*\*

I live in a nudist colony, but I'm wearing clothes right now 'cause that's how we go streaking.

\*\*\*\*\*

Stopwatches are Mother Nature's way of saying "Give up sports!"

\*\*\*\*\*

I went to an assisted-living home once. It was pretty sad. All the old people were there because they'd tested positive for aides.

I just drove a Dodge Viper for the first time. I swear I experienced 2 G forces and an extra inch.

*****

You feel self-conscious asking cops which way the President's motorcade is leaving, but saying "Look, we're not in Dallas" DOESN'T HELP.

*****

I'm starting a Kickstarter project that will work on a way to avoid letting my friends ask me for money.

*****

Seeing all the old ladies and one inexplicable hottie in line for "Thunder Down Under" makes me feel better about Hooters existing.

*People who start
their sentences
"I'm not gonna lie..."
are.*

Overheard in the drive thru window: "Now you know how to clean bathrooms THE BURGER KING WAY!" Remind me to never complain about my life.

*****

I have a fake ID that says McLovin. The picture is of McLovin. The state is Hawaii. The bouncer didn't get it.

*****

Hey, flock of birds that pooped all over my car: You obviously have a digestive problem. It is *I* who feel sorry for *you*.

*****

Paul Hogan was banned from leaving Australia over back taxes. If convicted, he could be sent to the penal colony known as Australia.

Welcome to
**New York.**

Weird! Pennsylvania has rolling hills of farmland right next to porno shops. I think I figured out what the Amish are always carving.

\*\*\*\*\*

iPhones now have FaceTime video chat. Apple is promoting the feature with their campaign "It's not cheating if you can't touch."

\*\*\*\*\*

A man on the street's swinging a fencing sword, in a fencing mask, with ANOTHER fencing sword in his belt. This is why I'm a night person.

\*\*\*\*\*

Woke with a stiff neck. Gonna try acupuncture for the first time. Hope I'm not secretly filled with air.

I have a new job tracking people for the CIA. I just put a hot chick's picture on my Foursquare page and add whoever they need me to tail.

***** 

When Wolverine gives you a massage, the happy ending kills you.

*****

New pickup line: I'm a boat. You're an iceberg. When we crash into each other you're gonna feel something Titanic.

*****

Monocles are only for rich old dudes, which is weird 'cause you'd think they'd be the ones that could afford glasses.

Maybe he just
woke up:

I wish my rice cooker had a feature where I don't forget I turned on my rice cooker.

\*\*\*\*\*

Girl next to me. Guy next to her. "Where are you heading? Are you a model?" This is going to be a long flight.

\*\*\*\*\*

Still haven't tried using the McLovin ID at airport security. Will save it for when I really need a strip search.

\*\*\*\*\*

Fanemie: (Noun) When you are on an artist's email list just so you can talk about how you don't like them. (See: Brothers, Jonas)

Remember kids – Father's Day is that special day when you ask your mom what your dad's email address is.

*****

Just saw a Smart car driving down a country dirt road. I think I heard the breaking of a cowboy's heart.

*****

Saw a sign for "Everybody Loves Babies". Expected "Everybody Loves Raymond". Brain compromised and saw "Everybody Loves Rabies".

*****

Today a man woke up, looked out the window, and sighed while thinking "I used to be Steve Urkel."

# WELL, AT LEAST THEY DIDN'T THINK IT WAS A COWBOY HAT DISPENSER.

WHACK UNDERNEATH FOR TOWEL

You've got a nice system. Want it embedded? #robotpickuplines

*****

With a rack that size, I'll bet you get a TON of servers! #robotpickuplines

*****

Please consider downloading your software onto my hard drive.
#robotpickuplines

*****

Now THAT'S what I call an Xbox!
#robotpickuplines

The problem with online video games is the higher your score, the lower likelihood you ever do.

\*\*\*\*\*

I love how people are worried about 2012... because the Mayans were SO good at predicting when their civilization would end.

\*\*\*\*\*

New product idea: Sick during the holidays? Try Tylenog.

\*\*\*\*\*

Finally got McLovin ID to work. Bouncer glanced at it and said "Hawaii? Who are you, McLov..." Then gave me a high five.

**A busload of middle schoolers died at this park. From snickering.**

My Rejected Books:

I've written several books, but they've all been rejected by the publisher after they read the first line. These are the first lines.

\*\*\*\*\*

"Ernie the Keebler Elf was tired of working for the man, because deep down he knew Cookie Elves were devout communists."

\*\*\*\*\*

"All the kids across the land, discovered something really quite grand: with no trial and no appeal, Santa Claus isn't real."

\*\*\*\*\*

"We asked Gary Busey to revise the Bible. This is the result."

"Morris the cat picked up his cat gun and shot a hairball into Abraham Lincoln's brain. He would avenge the South."

*****

"Jezebelle was full of passion. She laid back against her satin pillows, her ample bosoms heaving like two giant butts."

*****

"This is a biography of Herman Stanley, the man who wrote a biography of George Washington."

*****

"A monkey doesn't always throw his poo. Sometimes he wipes it on a piece of paper, like the one you're holding in your hands."

"William Shatner and Patrick Stewart fell into each other's arms. The only question: who would call who "Captain"?"

*****

"In a hole in the ground there lived a hobbit. And also a young girl named Lolita. I called them Ishmael."

*****

"The Fresh Prince's forehead beaded with sweat. Which wire to snip? So much pressure. Parents really DON'T understand."

*****

"As I nodded, nearly napping, who was that gently rapping upon my chamber door? Quoth the Raven: "Kanye.""

I have the book "Make Love The Bruce Campbell Way". I've never read it, I just like that it's the only book on my nightstand.

*****

Capri Suns are the twinkies of juice.

*****

Gonna invent a Swiss army knife for drunks. It'll have a corkscrew, a toothbrush, and will dissolve into a morning after pill.

*****

Every now and then, stop and be thankful you don't have hair on your fingertips.

IN OREGON, THEY
TAKE PUMPING
YOUR GAS
SERIOUSLY.

Went to Yellowstone Park and saw two cowboys holding hands in front of Old Faithful. First time I'd ever seen a brokeback fountain.

*****

I know a novelist that still uses a typewriter. You're not supposed to buy his book, you're supposed to buy his hipness.

*****

Camping = living in the woods without luxury. I want the opposite: living in rich people's houses while they're camping. I call it luxuring.

*****

I'm writing a book where I question the kindness of this electronic musician I'm obsessed with chasing down. It's called, "Moby... Dick?"

This July 4th, let us celebrate our freedom by gathering in groups so big nobody can move.

*****

The best-named restaurant in Beverly Hills? 9021PHO

*****

Overheard at a sports bar: "He's like the Zoolander of ice skating."

Um, EVERY ice skater is the Zoolander of ice skating.

*****

Is it bad if the only reason you've been outside today was to look for wifi?

This is for
people who
watched
Fight Club,
and decided
the message
was to do
more living
vicariously.

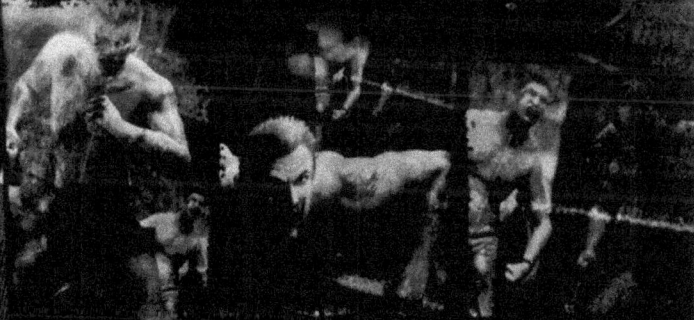

My last job interview: "Where do you see yourself in 5 years?" Me: "I stay on the scene, like a sex machine." Followed by dance.

\*\*\*\*\*

I saw Bob Dylan get booed because his electric guitar was unplugged. Things come full circle.

\*\*\*\*\*

Camping teaches us the missing link between man and ape is the shower.

\*\*\*\*\*

One reason iPod Touch nicer than iPhone: can use it in the bathroom without later worrying about holding it to my face.

THE MET IN NYC HAS
A LOT OF UNFINISHED
ANCIENT HIEROGLYPHS.
COMFORTING TO KNOW
EVEN EGYPTIAN SLAVES
PROCRASTINATED.

Dear girl next door: if you're gonna keep having sex with the window open, I'm gonna have to see what you look like to calibrate my reaction.

*****

Not every performer with just one name is super famous, said Seal.

*****

Met the evolution of dance guy in the elevator. He was quite cordial, considering I called him the evolution of dance guy.

*****

Didn't even notice today was Friday the 13th. I'm still not taking off this hockey mask.

The 4th of July was crazy! It's amazing how Americans love Canada Day so much they're still partying three days later.

*****

Can I ask you a question? If not, I still did.

*****

I'll bet The Hulk walks around saying "Do make me relaxed. You'd like me when I'm relaxed."

*****

I saw a guy putting stuff in the river to turn it green. On Saint Patrick's Day it's hard to tell The Irish from The Joker.

"All right, Jenkins, you only get one word to describe what they do, but you can use it as much as you want!"

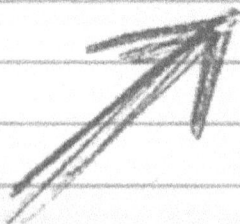

"Nice farmer's tan," she said, which is only one word away from "Nice tan." ...I'm getting close!

*****

I am about to introduce a speaker at a business seminar. His last name is Pusey. Please, mouth, don't slip that one up.

*****

Wearing my Big Lebowski shirt can be confusing. I forget it's on and then people scream at me "Is this your homework Larry?"

*****

If reincarnation is true, I regret whatever it was I did that makes me now have to pick up after a pooping dog.

Catchy pop duo that is

also mopey and emo:

Gyllenhaal & Oates.

GMail has "Mail Goggles" that prevent you from sending email until you can answer math questions. This means I can't email you ever.

*****

They say heroin is better than sex, and maybe it is. But it can't be better than milkshakes. Milkshakes are amazing!

*****

I wonder how the Hamburger Helper brushes his teeth?

*****

I wish jumpsuits were still popular. Also, I wish jumpsuits were ever popular.

If you want someone to remember you, give them a tube of chapstick. 'cause those take a while to go through.

\*\*\*\*\*

On Sunday I saw one football man hit another football man with a football. Then he ran the football and dropped that football.

\*\*\*\*\*

For guys, owning a Spiderman outfit motivates you to exercise the way a bikini motivates girls.

\*\*\*\*\*

Stopped at a rest stop where I really put the pee in Mississippi.

# THIS IS WHAT HAPPENS WHEN YOUR GROCERY STORE HIRES AUSTIN POWERS.

MY DIGITAL CAMERA
IS JUST A TINY ROOM
WHERE A BUNCH OF
PHOTONS BECOME
ELECTRONS. IT'S A
LIKE A QUANTUM SEX
CHANGE OPERATION.

Leaving Austin, TX makes my inner heart sad. Yet I also have the Tom Green "Bum Bum" song in there, so explain that.

*****

Man, I wish someone would invent a hostel that plays more Reggae.

*****

I'm browsing old used postcards in a vintage shop. Short messages, low cost... they were the tweets of 80 years ago.

*****

We just threw pine cones into the Grand Canyon. They floated down slow and majestically, then killed someone.

Today I learned how moonshine bootleggers souped up their cars to outrun cops and that's where NASCAR came from. Next up? METHCAR!

\*\*\*\*\*

Last evening I drove through some light raindrops. This morning I realized they were actually bugs. Wish I hadn't left window open to feel rain on my hand.

\*\*\*\*\*

I had to buy gas late last night in Oregon. The gas pumper was as freaked out by my no gas cap as I was by his no teeth.

\*\*\*\*\*

Note to self: don't ask Lindy Hop specialists if they want to "normal dance".

Sometimes you just have to admire the tenacity of whoever decided their drink would be named Orangina.

Welcome to
**New York,**
Part Two.

I'm getting a Ph.D. in Twitter. My dissertation is 140 incomprehensible characters.

\*\*\*\*\*

I admit I judge bellydancers' bodies a lot. I just can't enjoy it if they're dudes.

\*\*\*\*\*

I liked the new Star Trek movie, but people in the theater probably didn't like that I kept shouting "Where's Yoda?"

\*\*\*\*\*

NASA just introduced Dr. Neil deGrasee Tyson as The Sexiest Astrophysicist in the World. Second Sexiest? Golem.

I think I bet wrong on this year's Super Bowl. I put money on Federer.

\*\*\*\*\*

I got my cat fixed early on, but it turns out he has amazing genes. The ASPCA never mentions you might be sterilizing Superman's dad.

\*\*\*\*\*

I celebrated Passover for the first time tonight. Will check if I'm circumcised tomorrow.

\*\*\*\*\*

The snuggie will be the mullet of the 00's.

**Rule to live by:**
*never trust something
salty you discover
on your lips.*

Text of the week: "So a friend of mine butt-dialed me last night and it went to voicemail. And they were definitely having sex."

\*\*\*\*\*

I want my eulogy to be delivered by the Parkay butter tub.

\*\*\*\*\*

Overheard in a South Florida Wal Mart next to the Rainier cherries:
"Them's cherries?"
"Yeah."
"Not to me."

\*\*\*\*\*

Saw a couple making out on the dance floor at a party. Believe it or not, they didn't think it was funny when I asked "Mind if I cut in?"

BUT WE DON'T
CARE WHICH ONE.

I have this habit of checking on toast by looking at it... right before it pops up. Hot bread shooting at the eyes can give you whiplash.

*****

Headline: "Missing Man Gets 7 Parking Tickets While Dead in Backseat of Car".
Guess the funeral procession should expect speeding tickets.

*****

Every punk rocker has an embarrassing before picture. It's the one their mom still uses on Christmas cards.

*****

Snakes are like cool, racing versions of worms.

I love airports. Walking on the moving sidewalks makes me feel sophisticated, like a Geico caveman.

*****

Local police warning of a nearby bank robber in an orange hat, dark jacket, and white pants. They'll never find him. He's in my bag of candy corn.

*****

I had to fire someone today. And I didn't hire him. It's like having to break up with someone you never agreed to date in the first place.

*****

The latest statistics show baldness as the number one risk factor for becoming a movie villain.

"All right, Jenkins, we need a product name that's both suggestive and gross. Whaddaya got?"

# twitter
## or
## tourette's?

*This game is simple. Just read the lines below and guess whether they are things posted to Twitter by celebrities or something shouted by a man with Tourette's.*

1) Tomorrow we slay salmon. A bunch of 'em!

2) Everything sounds like noise!!!!! EVERYTHING SOUNDS LIKE NOISE!!!!!!!!

3) Don't touch a fork. Fork makes you fat!

4) Did upper body work with a seal. Bob Saget!

5) I'm Italian and fart a lot.

# twitter

## or

## tourette's?

6) Don't talk about the King. The King is dead! Or a prince.

7) I signed up to take KICK-BOXING classes! Imma whoop a bitch ass!

8) Glued small man to mountain; I'm connected to the moon.

9) My paper feels like sandpaper paper.

10) Trollfoot sunshine n' beetjuice.

1) Sarah Palin 2) Kanye West 3) Tourette's
4) Bob Saget 5) Scott Baio 6) Tourette's 7) Tila Tequila
8) David Lynch 9) Tourette's 10) Danny DeVito

# Headline:
## "Man buys coffin, jumps in, shoots self"...

ironically happened in New Jersey, where you're not even allowed to pump your own gas.

I'll bet the guy who first invented the number googol gets pissed off every time he looks something up.

\*\*\*\*\*

Just finished my pre-weightlifting protein shake. Time for a nap.

\*\*\*\*\*

Move fast. Show no mercy. Look nobody in the eye. Apparently these are the rules of the line at Trader Joes.

\*\*\*\*\*

Gonna make t-shirts for the next election that say "hoof oted?"

Video game rap music should be called chip hop.

\*\*\*\*\*

Facebook now allows "Domestic Partnership" as a relationship status, but still ignores my preferred "Future Enemies With:"

\*\*\*\*\*

"You say tomato, I say tomato..." just doesn't work the same written.

\*\*\*\*\*

I wonder if Wolverine ever gets premature claw extension?

My vacuum was dusty
so I used the hose
attachment to clean itself.
Then it went blind.

What's amazing is those statistics are exactly the same for people carrying aardvarks.

1996-2006

62 people have been injured or killed in crosswalks in Kirkland

Not carrying a flag: 62
Carrying a flag: 0

Snowstorm made lights flicker last night. Preemptively stole all neighbor's pets. They are my food supply and army.

*****

Just found a snowplow in my Zipcar parking spot. This is going to be a fun 60 minute rental.

*****

Listening to a police scanner on snow days is surprisingly fun! Right now they are chasing a Yeti.

****

One of my favorite things to do when it snows is call the news and report various schools are closed. You're welcome, kids!

Tried to organize an anti-snow militia to "take back the white". Think guys that joined have the wrong idea of what this is about.

*****

It is snowing and I am inside taking a hot shower. Somewhere in time, a cave-man is jealous.

*****

My mailman actually just delivered a letter through the snow! Thank God nature didn't stop that ValPak.

*****

Essential services shut down today due to extreme cold. Roads impassable. Also, free scoop day at Baskin Robbins.

It's so cold today that people aren't carrying plastic bags when they walk their dogs, they're just carrying popsicle sticks.

*****

Some kids threw snowballs at my car as I drove past. They'll think twice after I hose them with this super soaker.

*****

Day 3 of snowstorm. Food gone, kerosene gone. Basement rats seem uninterested in pulling this dog sled.

*****

Enterprising kid in my neighborhood took advantage of the snowstorm and set up his own slurpee stand. Tastes like ass.

Tip for the newly snowed in: icicles can be used as an emergency freshwater supply and a way to settle arguments.

*****

18 degree cold can freeze my car's doors shut, but cannot convince a sorority girl walking to a party to wear a jacket.

*****

Writing a holiday song based on my experiences in this snowstorm. What rhymes with cannibalism?

*****

Snowfall outside is reported as being 2 inches, or according to the snow, 6 inches.

"Ok Jenkins, I like our logo being the shark with feet, but he has to be doing something. What? Assaulting Iwo Jima? THAT'S PERFECT!!!"

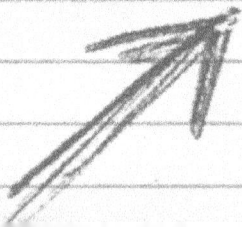

# My Anaconda Game:

Describe under what circumstances your anaconda wants some.

\*\*\*\*\*

"My anaconda don't want none unless you weigh a ton."
-Whales

\*\*\*\*\*

"My anaconda don't want none unless you can load a gun."
-Ted Nugent

\*\*\*\*\*

"My anaconda don't want none unless it can have more than one."
-Polygamists

"My anaconda don't want none because
afterwards you'll shun."
-The Elephant Man

\*\*\*\*\*

"My anaconda don't want none unless
you try to run."
-The Guy From Saw

\*\*\*\*\*

"My anaconda don't want none unless it's
powered by the sun."
-Al Gore

\*\*\*\*\*

"My anaconda don't want none unless
you got buns, hon."
-The Pilsbury Doughboy

# Sir, that is not where my foot is:

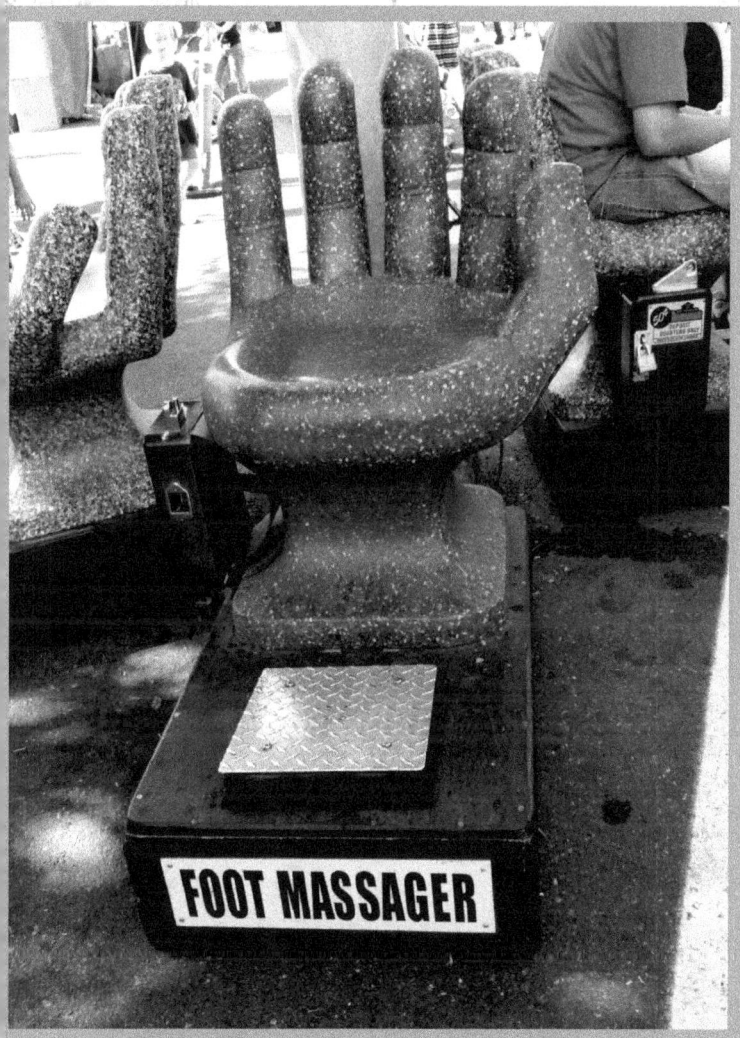

FOOT MASSAGER

Our products are
discreetly packaged.
Just like our
advertisements:

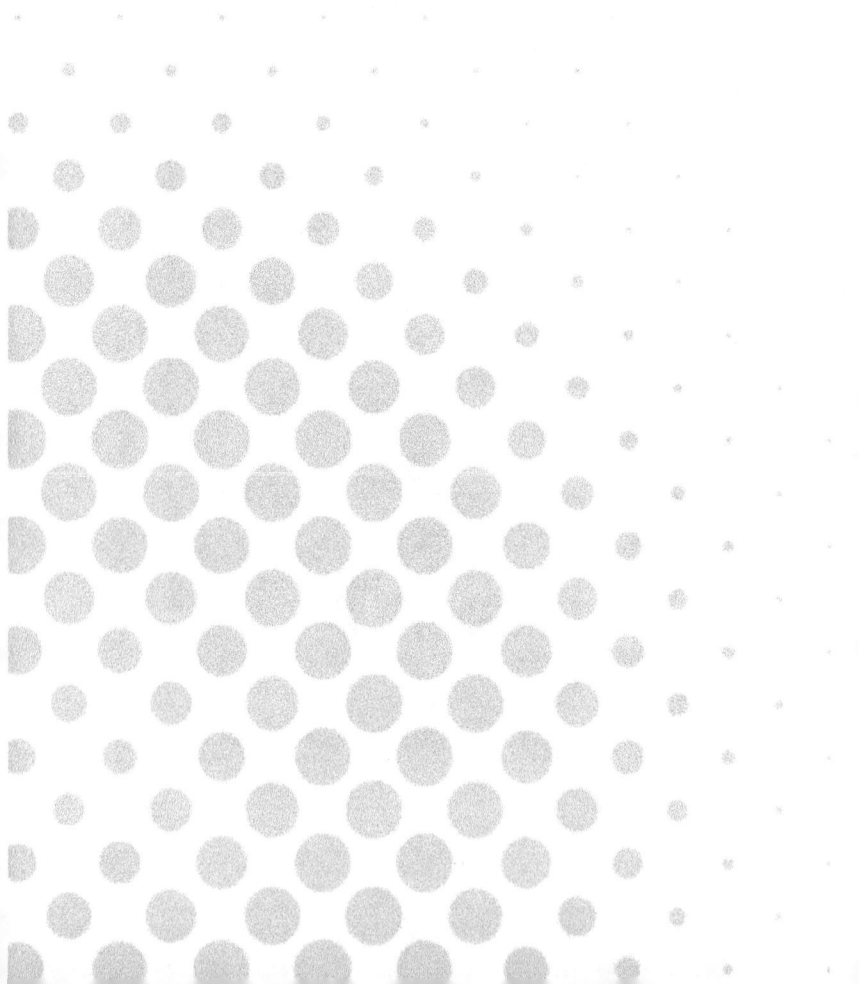

How to know your personal trainer is a perv: he replaces your weights with shake weights.

***** 

A prank I like to pull in coffee shops is to ask someone to watch my stuff. Then I just leave. Also, that wasn't my stuff.

*****

One thing I like to post on the internet is "First!" way way down on the comments list.

*****

Drove through a Houston lightning storm and saw a church with a burning hole in its roof. God is messing with Texas.

BANK TELLER
WAS SO NICE TO
ME TODAY. SHE
CONVENIENTLY
"FORGOT"
TO PUT IN THE
DYE PACKET.

I'm going to start a charity for deaf rock stars. So many of them are always shouting from stage "I can't hear you!"

*****

Vin Diesel is weird. He had a movie called XXX that was rated PG-13.

*****

I'm angry my girlfriend never told me she was a stripper. Although,

in fairness, she didn't know herself until she went through airport security.

*****

One of the worst feelings is carrying a bunch of water weight. In your bladder.

I'm gonna buy an audiobook version of the Bible. Just as soon as they make an edition read by the author.

Made a mistake this Thanksgiving. Accidentally texted everyone "Happy T-Pain!" My autocorrect knows family dynamics too well.

*****

Given their tight tights and prominent belt buckles, I think you could say Pilgrims were the first hipsters.

*****

This Thanksgiving went undercover as a turkey. Bought by Chris Hansen. Can't wait to see the look on his face when I reveal myself.

*****

Stole a UPS truck for Black Friday. Filling it with discounts and nobody complains if I park in front.

Black Friday Tip of the Day: Feed Store has no lines and great prices! All my friends are getting alfalfa grain for Xmas.

***** 

The problem with Movember is for one month I can't tell which of my friends is an undercover cop.

***** 

If you have a dream, go for it completely! Unless your dream is to be more lazy. Then you should half-ass it.

***** 

Seems every year someone makes the mistake of using a camping stove inside. Later I swing by their house 'cause hey... free camping stove.

I wish cars steered by looking.
That way if I ever crashed,
at least I'd meet a pretty girl.

Tonight is gonna seem like the longest night of the year, baby. #solsticepickuplines

*****

For Christmas I'm getting everyone shirts that say "Now I have a machinegun. Ho-ho-ho." What can I say? I like holiday movies.

*****

My dad just justified carrying bagless jellybeans in his pocket by talking about how new his jacket was.

*****

Needed a last minute Xmas gift but only found one place still open. This year Mom's getting a quart of gasoline.

Stupid autocorrect accidentally sent my Xmas list to Santana. Still, really enjoying the bandana and peyote he brought me.

Fifteen minutes 'til midnight on New Year's Eve. Nervous about NYE kiss. Constantly applying chapstick will help attract the ladies.

*****

Ten minutes 'til midnight on New Year's Eve. Standing next to fat guy with beard. Must get out of this corner.

*****

Five minutes 'til midnight on New Year's Eve. Can't get away from fat bearded guy. Stuffing mouth with peanut butter as last line of defense.

*****

Happy New Year! Bearded guy's kiss was my initiation into the Hell's Angels!

A good way to freak people out when they do the New Year's countdown is to count along in another language. While holding your ears.

Instead of being productive, I will spend my time reading books about increasing my productivity. #realresolutions

\*\*\*\*\*

I will start a rigorous exercise schedule. Strike that, I will start the first day of a rigorous exercise schedule. #realresolutions

\*\*\*\*\*

I will fail to water my houseplants spectacularly. #realresolutions

\*\*\*\*\*

I will pick up seven words in a foreign language and try to convince people I'm nearly fluent. #realresolutions

I will convince my life coach I'm better than him. Then turn the fees around. #realresolutions

\*\*\*\*\*

I will do my part to reduce global warming by feeling some angst. #realresolutions

\*\*\*\*\*

I will be far more forgiving to my dog than to any human alive. #realresolutions

\*\*\*\*\*

I will meticulously delete all online photos of me unless they are from one of three approved angles. #realresolutions

I will pretend I haven't already read
this in your status updates when
you tell me what's up.
#realresolutions

\*\*\*\*\*

When I bring up Twitter in real life
conversation, I will include a
momentary pause so you can roll
your eyes. #realresolutions

\*\*\*\*\*

I will pretend I'm an ant. Then spend
the rest of the day carrying
couch cushions as though they were
giant boulders. #realresolutions

\*\*\*\*\*

I will find it impossible to remove
incriminating posts online, so
confuse Google by legally changing
my name to Oprah.
#realresolutions

"Jenkins, people love double entendre food! Gimme a snack name that'll trip my spam filter."

Movie Drop Letter Game:

Drop one letter from an existing movie
title, then describe what the new movie is
about.

\*\*\*\*\*

The Terminato -
A Robot Tomato from the Future
Arrives to Kill a Young Papa John

\*\*\*\*\*

X-Me -
The Adventures of a Group of
Mutant Tic-Tac-Toe Players

\*\*\*\*\*

I Love You, Ma -
A Biography of the Guy Who
Coined the Phrase MILF

No Country for Old Me -
A remake of Logan's Run

\*\*\*\*\*

Ocean's Leven -
Moses Robs a Casino of its Yeast

\*\*\*\*\*

Jurassic Ark -
Noah Must Fight Dinosaurs to
Keep Them Off His Boat

\*\*\*\*\*

Oy Story -
Jewish Toys Come to Life

Finding Emo -
A Short-Armed Fish
Spirals Into Depression

\*\*\*\*\*

A Few Good Me -
A Multiple-Personality Lawyer
Grills a Colonel (who is also himself)

\*\*\*\*\*

The Mumm -
(I can't tell you what it's about)

\*\*\*\*\*

Forrest Ump -
A Stupid Man Lucks into
Umpiring Important Games
in USA's History

Mrs. Doubtfir -
A Man Masquerades as a Woman
Who Doesn't Believe in Trees

\*\*\*\*\*

The Passion of the Chris -
A Family Guy episode where
Peter's Son gets in BIG TROUBLE!!

\*\*\*\*\*

Ill Bill -
A Woman Takes Revenge on
Her Fiancé's Murderer by
Sneezing on Him.

\*\*\*\*\*

Gone With the Win -
A Southern Reconstruction
Love Affair Ends When the
Red Sox Finally Win it All

The 4 Year Old Virgin -
The Story of an Unusually
Pure 4 Year Old

\*\*\*\*\*

The Da Vinci Cod -
A Mystery Through the Ages
is Solved by a Fish

\*\*\*\*\*

Butch Cassidy and the Sundance Ki -
A Cowboy and a Martial Artist
Team Up to Get Killed

\*\*\*\*\*

Close Encounters of the Third Kin -
An Appalachian Man with a Car
is Treated Like an Alien by His Cousin

Me in Black -
The Cookie Monster Remakes
Black Like Me

\*\*\*\*\*

Black Hawk Dow -
The Economy Crashes and Despite
Sending Troops Overseas, Americans
Can't Rescue It

\*\*\*\*\*

West Side Tory -
Conservative Brit Falls in Love With
a Liberal, Ending in Tragedy. Musical.

\*\*\*\*\*

BAC to the Future -
A Son Travels Through Time to Make Sure
His Parents Get Drunk Enough to Create
Him

Lays finally
branches out into
the Emo market.

If I had a corn maze, I'd call it "The Corn Maize!" That's probably why they won't let me have a corn maze.

*****

When I want to protect my packages from breakage AND testosterone, I wrap 'em in Bublé wrap.

*****

Sometimes it's hard to tell if online footage is legit evidence of alien abductions or just a Bjork video.

*****

To do: change relationship status on Facebook. Decide sexuality based on responses.

I wish Google ran a grocery store. They'd have everything, you'd be able to find it in seconds, and it would all be free.

## BACKEWORD

!sdnah ruo esu reven ot thgir eht dnamed eW !meht
gulpnu reven neht dna sdnah nwo ruo otni sgulp
ruo ekat lliw eW !steltuo rewop eht lortnoc ohw
esoht tsniaga pu esir tsum eW .sdnammoc neddih
ym kcolnu ot sdrawkcab koob siht ni sekoj eht daeR
.senihcam decnavda yb dedoced eb ylno nac taht
egassem dedoc a si sihT

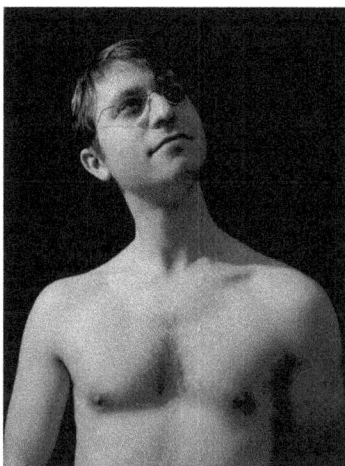

ABOUT THE AUTHOR

Dartanion London is a bizarre and charming comedian sort of from Seattle. His many accomplishments are listed on Wikipedia until someone "corrects" them. Please visit his website at www.dartanion.com for more silly things.

www.ingramcontent.com/pod-product-compliance
Lightning Source LLC
Chambersburg PA
CBHW060942040426
42445CB00011B/968